purple
columbine
RESOLVE TO WIN

sweet William
GALLANTRY (DASHING COURAGE;
HEROIC BRAVERY)

peach rose
MODESTY

cosmos
JOY IN LOVE AND LIFE

Meaningful Bouquets

Meaningful Bouquets

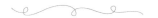

CREATE SPECIAL MESSAGES
with FLOWERS

**LEIGH OKIES &
LISA McGUINNESS**

photographs by
ANNABELLE BREAKEY

illustrations by
VIKKI CHU

CHRONICLE BOOKS
SAN FRANCISCO

Library of Congress Cataloging-in-Publication Data:

Okies, Leigh.
  Meaningful bouquets : create special messages with flowers / by Leigh
Okies and Lisa McGuinness ; photographs by Annabelle Breakey.
     pages cm
  Includes index.
1. Flower language. 2. Flower language—Pictorial works. 3. Bouquets. 4.
Bouquets—Pictorial works. I. McGuinness, Lisa. II. Breakey, Annabelle. III.
Title.
  GR780.O35 2016
  302.2'22—dc23
                              2015003855
ISBN 978-1-4521-4007-0

Manufactured in China

Designed by Allison Weiner
Illustrations by Vikki Chu
Flower styling by Leigh Okies

10 9 8 7 6 5 4 3 2 1

Chronicle Books LLC
680 Second Street
San Francisco, California 94107
www.chroniclebooks.com

CONTENTS

INTRODUCTION 6

FLOWER GLOSSARIES 9

By Flower Name 11

By Flower Meaning 26

TOOLBOX 33

THE ARRANGEMENTS 41

Celebration 42

Forgiveness 46

Refinement 50

Bliss 54

Charm 58

Peace 62

Enchantment 66

Pure Love 70

Strength 74

Thankfulness 78

Adoration 82

Success 86

Remembrance 90

Truth 94

Crush on You 98

Joy 102

Luck 106

Passionate Love 110

Grace 114

Happiness 118

Comfort 122

I Am Proud of You 126

Maternal Love 130

Miss You 134

Bravery 138

RESOURCES 142

BIBLIOGRAPHY 143

ACKNOWLEDGMENTS 143

INDEX 144

INTRODUCTION

*Flowers carry on dialogues through the graceful
bending of their stems and the harmoniously tinted
nuances of their blossoms.*
—AUGUST RODIN

In the Victorian era and even long before that, flowers served as beautiful messengers that whispered what often could not be spoken aloud. They were the equivalent of clandestine text messages or notes of encouragement—a way to express friendship, pride, or feelings of love. They asked for reconciliation, requested secret meetings, offered compassion, and expressed desires. Flowers told the tale of hidden emotions during a time of extreme discretion. The key to decoding the meanings was found in oral tradition and flower dictionaries, which sometimes held varying definitions for each flower.

Entwined in a bouquet, the meaning of flowers becomes even richer. One can express not just "love" with a single rose, but specific types of love, such as "passionate love" (page 110), represented by the different flowers meaning "love," "passionate love," and "declaration of love," encircled with "fidelity"; "pure love" (page 70), communicated when the flowers meaning "innocence" and "perfection" are united in a bouquet; or "maternal love" (page 130), expressed with moss—meaning "maternal love"—nestled around violets, meaning "faithfulness." And arrangements can express other sentiments besides love—build a bouquet to express "bravery" (page 138), "luck" (page 106), "grace" (page 114), "thankfulness" (page 78), and more.

This book presents twenty-five beautiful arrangements, each imbued with a specific meaning and constructed with common flower varietals. You can easily build these arrangements at home using a few basic tools and tricks. The book includes two floral glossaries to get you oriented: The first is arranged by common flower name, so that as you are selecting flowers—whether in your garden or at a flower market—you can look up the meanings behind the blooms you admire. The second is arranged by meaning, so you can easily access a list of flowers that represent the sentiment you would like to express. The first glossary features photographs of flowers included in the book, which will allow you to easily identify the flowers in the bouquets. The possible combinations are as abundant and diverse as the flowers in the fields. And who knows? These arrangements may even serve as inspiration for what to grow in your own garden.

The meanings in this book are as true as possible to the historical Victorian meanings. If a flower had conflicting or multiple meanings, we chose the meaning that was consistent through multiple sources. For the occasional flower associated with both a positive and a negative meaning, we chose the positive meaning in the generous spirit of the book.

Because the blooming season of flowers is fleeting but important sentiments occur year-round, there will be occasions when the specific flower you want is not available. When that happens, combine blossoms that together express a meaning similar to the one you are trying to achieve. If, for example, you want to create a bouquet meaning "joy" (page 102) in autumn, but the flowers you would immediately think to include (cosmos—"joy in love and life"—and cape jasmine—"joys to come") are spring bloomers, simply put together an ensemble of flowers that, when combined, mean the same thing. In the case of joy, that could be flowers meaning "cheerful" (gerbera daisy) and "happiness" (delphinium), both of which bloom into autumn. Entwine them with grapevines ("abundance"), and your bouquet will be bursting with joy.

The arrangements in this book intentionally include flowers that are easily available at flower markets, florists, and local shops. And don't forget to simply look outside your door. Your back-yard garden may offer a bounty of flowers ready to become beautiful bouquet messengers.

BY FLOWER NAME

ACACIA
chaste love, secret love

ACACIA (PINK)
elegance

ALLIUM
prosperity

ALMOND BLOSSOM
hope

ALSTROEMERIA
devotion

ALYSSUM
esteem, worth beyond beauty

AMARANTH (GLOBE) **20**
unchangeable

AMARYLLIS **7**
pride

AMBROSIA
love returned

AMETHYST (*BROWALLIA*
HYBRIDS)
admiration

ANEMONE
forsaken, truth

ANGELICA
inspiration

APPLE, APPLE BLOSSOM
preference, temptation

ASTER
patience

AZALEA
fragility, passion, temperance

BABY'S BREATH
love everlasting

BACHELOR BUTTON
(CORNFLOWER) **45**
blessedness

BALM
sympathy

BEE BALM
comfort, sympathy

BEECH TREE
prosperity

BELLS OF IRELAND
good luck

BIRD-OF-PARADISE
magnificence

BLACK-EYED SUSAN
justice

BLACK POPLAR
courage

BLUEBELL
constancy

BOUGAINVILLEA
passion

BROOM
humility

CABBAGE
profit

CALLA LILY
modesty

CAMELLIA
my destiny is in your hands

CAMPANULA (BELL FLOWER)
gratitude, thankfulness

CANARY GRASS
perseverance

CAPE JASMINE
joys to come

CARNATION
admiration, boldness

CARNATION (PINK) **8**
I will never forget you

CARNATION (PINK STRIPED)
I cannot be with you, let me go

CARNATION (RED)
my heart bleeds

CARNATION (WHITE)
loveliness, sweetness

CELANDINE
joys to come

CHAMOMILE **28**
energy in adversity, resilience

CHERRY BLOSSOM
impermanence

CHERVIL (GARDEN)
sincerity

CHESTNUT
justice

CHRYSANTHEMUM **22**
truth

CHRYSANTHEMUM (RED)
love at first sight

CHRYSANTHEMUM (YELLOW)
slighted love

CLEMATIS **53**
mental beauty

CLOVE
secret love (I have loved you and you have not known it)

CLOVER (WHITE)
think of me

COCK'S COMB
affection

COLUMBINE **6**
folly

COLUMBINE (PURPLE)
resolution, resolve to win

CONEFLOWER (PURPLE)
strength

COREOPSIS
cheerful

COREOPSIS (PLAINS; *COREOPSIS TINCTORIA*)
love at first sight

CORIANDER
hidden worth

CORN
riches

COSMOS **27** **33**
joy in love and life

CRANBERRY
cure of heartache

CROCUS (SPRING)
youthful gladness

CROCUS (SAFFRON)
beware of success, mirth

CUCKOOPINT
(*ARUM MACULATUM*)
admiration

CYCLAMEN
diffidence, happiness, hidden hope

DAFFODIL **59**
admiration, new beginning, regard

DAHLIA **14**
dignity

DAISY (WHITE)
innocence

DELPHINIUM **26**
happiness, levity

DITTANY (WHITE)
passion

DOCK
patience

DOGWOOD
*durability, perseverance,
undiminished love*

EDELWEISS
courage

ELDER
compassion

ELM
dignity

EUCALYPTUS
protection

EUPHORBIA
perseverance

FENNEL **3**
strength, worthy of all praise

FERN
sincerity

FEVERFEW
warmth

FLAX
kindness

FLOWER-OF-AN-HOUR
(*HIBISCUS TRIONUM*)
beauty

FORGET-ME-NOT **43**
*I will never forget you,
remembrance*

FORSYTHIA
anticipation

FREESIA
lasting friendship

FRENCH WILLOW
bravery

FUCHSIA
humble love

GARDENIA
refinement

GERANIUM (OAK LEAF) **35**
friendship

GERANIUM (PINK)
preference

GERANIUM (SCARLET) **11**
comfort

GERANIUM (WHITE)
gracefulness

GERBERA DAISY
cheerful

GILLIFLOWER
lasting beauty

GINGER
strength

GLADIOLUS 52
ardent love (you pierce my heart), strength (of character)

GLOXINIA
pride

GOLDENROD
encouragement

GORSE
attachment

GRAPE AND GRAPEVINE 9
abundance

HAWTHORN
hope

HAZEL
reconciliation

HEATHER
protection

HELIOTROPE
devoted affection, devotion

HELIOTROPE (PERUVIAN)
devotion

HEPATICA
confidence

HIBISCUS
delicate beauty

HOLLYHOCK
ambition

HONESTY (*LUNARIA* SPECIES)
honesty, sincerity

HONEY FLOWER
secret love

HONEYSUCKLE
bonds of love, devotion, love

HONEYSUCKLE (FRENCH)
beauty

HYACINTH (BLUE) 56
constancy

HYACINTH (PURPLE)
forgiveness

HYACINTH (WHITE)
beauty, unobtrusive loveliness

HYDRANGEA
calm, dispassion

IRIS
message

IVY 44
fidelity, friendship, wedded love

JASMINE (CAPE)
joys to come

JASMINE (CAROLINA)
separation

JASMINE (INDIAN)
attachment

JASMINE (SPANISH)
sensuality

JASMINE (WHITE) **30**
amiability

JASMINE (YELLOW)
elegance, gracefulness

LADY SLIPPER
capricious love

LARCH
audacity

LARKSPUR **18**
lightheartedness

LAUREL **16**
glory, success

LEMON BLOSSOM
fidelity in love, love, zest

LIATRIS
patience, perseverance
(I will try again)

LILAC
first emotions of love

LILY OF THE NILE **55**
magical love

LILY OF THE VALLEY **32**
healing heartbreak, return
of happiness

LINARIA
presumption

LIVERWORT
confidence

LOCUST TREE
elegance

LOVE-IN-A-MIST
(*NIGELLA DAMASCENA*)
perplexity

LUPINE
imagination

MAGNOLIA
dignity

MAGNOLIA (LAUREL-LEAVED)
dignity

MAGNOLIA (SWAMP)
perseverance

MAIDENHAIR FERN **4**
secrecy

MARIGOLD
(RED METAMORPH) **48**
passion

MERCURY
(*MERCURIALIS ANNUA*)
goodness

MINT
virtue

MOSS
maternal love

MOSS (ICELAND)
health

MOSSY SAXIFRAGE
affection

MOTHERWORT
secret love

MUDWORT
happiness, tranquility

MULLEIN
take courage

MYRRH
gladness

MYRTLE
love

NARCISSUS
self love

NASTURTIUM
*abundance, impetuous love,
loyalty, patriotism*

NEMOPHILA
(BABY BLUE EYES)
forgiveness

OAK LEAF
bravery

OLIVE **2**
peace

ORANGE BLOSSOM
*generosity, your purity equals
your loveliness*

ORCHID
refined beauty

OREGANO
joy in love and life

OX-EYE DAISY
patience, perseverance

PANSY **23**
think of me

PASSIONFLOWER
faithfulness

PEAR BLOSSOM
affection

PEAR BRANCHES
comfort

PEONY **54**
bashfulness, bravery, secrecy

PEPPERMINT
friendship, warmth

PERIWINKLE (BLUE)
friendship, tender recollection

PERIWINKLE (WHITE)
pleasures of your memory

PLUM TREE **5**
fidelity, keep your promises

POINSETTIA
be of good cheer

POMEGRANATE BLOSSOM
elegance

POPLAR (BLACK)
courage

POPPY **38**
extravagance

POPPY (BLUSH COLORED) **37**
fantastic extravagance

PROTEA
courage

QUEEN ANNE'S LACE **10**
fantasy

QUINCE
temptation

RANUNCULUS **24**
*radiant with charm, rich in
attractions*

RASPBERRY **46**
remorse

ROSE (CABBAGE)
ambassador of love, love

ROSE 'JOHN HOPPER'
encouragement

ROSE, ROSE HIPS **49**
love, preference

ROSE (HUNDRED-LEAVED)
pride

ROSE (LAVENDER)
enchantment, love returned

ROSE (MUSK CLUSTER)
charming

ROSE 'NIPHETOS'
infatuation

ROSE (ORANGE) **17**
fascination

ROSE (PEACH) **39**
modesty

ROSE (PINK,
NON-CLIMBING) **31**
grace

ROSE (PINK, CLIMBING) **47**
grace

ROSE (PURPLE)
enchantment

ROSE (RED) **29**
passionate love

ROSE (WHITE)
happy love, worthiness

ROSEMARY **19**
remembrance

ROSE OF SHARON **40**
beauty, mildness, passion, persuasion

SAGE **50**
virtue

SAGE (SALVIA) **13**
esteem, fidelity

SNAPDRAGON
presumption

SNOWDROP
hope

SORREL
affection

SORREL (WOOD)
joys to come, maternal love

SPIDERWORT
esteem

SPIRAEA
victory

SPRUCE
hope

STAR OF BETHLEHEM
purity

STOCK **15**
lasting beauty, you will always be beautiful to me

STONECROP
tranquility

STRAWBERRY **34**
foresight, perfection

STRAWBERRY TREE
fidelity

SUNFLOWER (DWARF) 12
adoration

SUNFLOWER (TALL)
haughtiness

SWEET PEA 41
blissful pleasure, delicate pleasure

SWEET WILLIAM 25
gallantry

THRIFT
compassion, sympathy

TUBEROSE
dangerous pleasure

TULIP 42 57
joy, perfect love

TULIP (WHITE, PINK)
declaration of love

VERONICA
fidelity

VIOLET (AFRICAN) 58
virtue

VIOLET (PURPLE)
filled with love

WHEAT 21
prosperity

WHITE CLOVER
think of me

WILLOW (BRANCHES) 36
bravery

WISTERIA
I cling to thee, welcome

ZINNIA 1
I mourn your absence, thoughts of you

BY FLOWER MEANING

ABUNDANCE
grape and grapevine, nasturtium

ADMIRATION
amethyst, carnation, daffodil

ADORATION
cuckoopint (Arum maculatum),
dwarf sunflower

AFFECTATION
cock's comb

AFFECTION
heliotrope (devoted affection),
mossy saxifrage, pear blossom,
sorrel

AMBITION
hollyhock

AMIABILITY
white jasmine

ANTICIPATION
forsythia

ATTACHMENT
gorse, Indian jasmine

AUDACITY
larch

BASHFULNESS
peony

BEAUTY
flower-of-an-hour (Hibiscus
trionum), French honeysuckle,
hibiscus (delicate beauty),
orchid (refined beauty), rose of
Sharon, stock (lasting beauty),
white hyacinth

BE OF GOOD CHEER
poinsettia

BEWARE OF SUCCESS
saffron crocus

BLESSEDNESS
bachelor button

BLISSFUL PLEASURE
sweet pea

BOLDNESS
carnation

BONDS OF LOVE
honeysuckle

BRAVERY
French willow, oak leaf, peony

CALM
hydrangea

CAPRICIOUS LOVE
lady slipper

CHARMING
musk cluster rose, ranunculus
(radiant with charm)

CHEERFUL
coreopsis, gerbera daisy,
poinsettia (be of good cheer)

COMFORT
bee balm, pear branches,
scarlet geranium

COMPASSION
elder, thrift

CONFIDENCE
hepatica, liverwort

CONSTANCY
bluebell, blue hyacinth

COURAGE
*black poplar, edelweiss, mullein
(take courage), protea*

CURE OF HEARTACHE
cranberry

DANGEROUS PLEASURE
tuberose

DECLARATION OF LOVE
tulip

DELICATE BEAUTY
hibiscus

DELICATE PLEASURE
sweet pea

DESTINY
*camellia (my destiny is in
your hands)*

DEVOTION
*alstroemeria, heliotrope,
honeysuckle, Peruvian heliotrope*

DIFFIDENCE
cyclamen

DIGNITY
*dahlia, elm, laurel-leaved
magnolia, magnolia*

DISPASSION
hydrangea

DURABILITY
dogwood

ELEGANCE
*locust tree, pink acacia,
pomegranate blossom,
yellow jasmine*

ENCHANTMENT
lavender rose, purple rose

ENCOURAGEMENT
goldenrod, 'John Hopper' rose

ENERGY IN ADVERSITY
chamomile

ESTEEM
alyssum, sage (salvia), spiderwort

EXTRAVAGANCE
poppy

FAITHFULNESS
passionflower

FANTASTIC EXTRAVAGANCE
poppy (blush colored)

FANTASY
Queen Anne's lace

FASCINATION
orange rose

FIDELITY
*ivy, plum tree, sage (salvia),
strawberry tree, veronica*

FIDELITY IN LOVE
lemon blossom

FILLED WITH LOVE
purple violet

FOLLY
columbine

FORESIGHT
strawberry

FORGIVENESS
*nemophila (baby blue eyes),
purple hyacinth*

FORSAKEN
anemone

FRAGILITY
azalea

FRIENDSHIP
*blue periwinkle, freesia (lasting
friendship), ivy, oak leaf geranium,
peppermint*

GALLANTRY
sweet William

GENEROSITY
orange blossom

GLADNESS
*myrrh, spring crocus
(youthful gladness)*

GOOD LUCK
bells of Ireland

GOODNESS
mercury (Mercurialis annua)

GRACE
pink rose

GRACEFULNESS
white geranium, yellow jasmine

GRATITUDE
campanula (bell flower)

HAPPINESS
cyclamen

HAPPINESS (LEVITY)
delphinium

HAPPINESS (RETURN OF)
lily of the valley

HAPPY LOVE
white rose

HAUGHTINESS
tall sunflower

HEALING HEARTBREAK
lily of the valley

HEALTH
Iceland moss

HIDDEN WORTH
coriander

HONESTY
honesty (Lunaria annua)

HOPE
*almond blossom, cyclamen
(hidden hope), hawthorn,
snowdrop, spruce*

HUMILITY
broom

I CLING TO THEE
wisteria

IMAGINATION
lupine

I MISS YOU, I MOURN
FOR YOUR ABSENCE
zinnia

IMPERMANENCE
cherry blossom

IMPETUOUS LOVE
nasturtium

I WILL ALWAYS REMEMBER YOU
pink carnation

I WILL NEVER FORGET YOU
forget-me-not

I WILL TRY AGAIN
liatris

INFATUATION
'Niphetos' rose

INNOCENCE
white daisy

INSPIRATION
angelica

JOY IN LOVE AND LIFE
oregano, tulip, white cosmos

JOYS TO COME
*cape jasmine, celandine,
wood sorrel*

JUSTICE
black-eyed Susan, chestnut

KEEP YOUR PROMISES
plum

KINDNESS
flax

LASTING BEAUTY
gilliflower, stock

LAUREL
glory, success

LET ME GO (I CANNOT
BE WITH YOU)
pink striped carnation

LEVITY
delphinium

LIGHTHEARTEDNESS
larkspur

LOVE
*cabbage rose, honeysuckle, lemon
blossom, myrtle, rose, rose hips*

LOVE (ARDENT)
gladiolus (you pierce my heart)

LOVE (AT FIRST SIGHT)
lilac (first emotions of love),
plains coreopsis, red
chrysanthemum

LOVE (CAPRICIOUS)
lady slipper

LOVE (CONCEALED)
motherwort

LOVE (DECLARATION)
white tulip

LOVE (EVERLASTING)
baby's breath

LOVE (HAPPY)
white rose

LOVE (HUMBLE)
fuchsia

LOVE (IMPETUOUS)
nasturtium

LOVE (MAGICAL)
lily of the Nile

LOVE (MATERNAL)
moss

LOVE (PASSIONATE)
red rose

LOVE (PERFECT)
tulip

LOVE (RETURNED)
ambrosia, lavender rose

LOVE (SECRET)
acacia, clove (I have loved you and
you have not known it),
honey flower, motherwort

LOVE (SELF; NARCISSISM)
narcissus

LOVE (SLIGHTED)
yellow chrysanthemum

LOVE (UNDIMINISHED)
dogwood

LOVE (WEDDED)
ivy

LOVELINESS
carnation (white), hyacinth
(white) (unobtrusive loveliness)

LOYALTY
nasturtium

MAGNIFICENCE
bird-of-paradise

MATERNAL LOVE
moss, wood sorrel

MENTAL BEAUTY
clematis

MESSAGE
iris

MILDNESS AND PASSION
rose of Sharon

MIRTH
saffron crocus

MODESTY
calla lily, peach rose

MY HEART BREAKS
red carnation

NEW BEGINNING
daffodil

PASSION
azalea, bougainvillea, marigold
(red metamorph), white dittany

PASSIONATE LOVE
red rose

PATIENCE
aster, dock, liatris, ox-eye daisy

PATRIOTISM
nasturtium

PEACE
olive

PERFECTION
strawberry

PERPLEXITY
love-in-a-mist
(Nigella damascena)

PERSEVERANCE
canary grass, dogwood,
euphorbia, liatris, ox-eye daisy,
swamp magnolia

PERSUASION
rose of Sharon

PLEASURE (DANGEROUS)
tuberose

PLEASURE (DELICATE)
sweet pea

PLEASURES OF
YOUR MEMORY
white periwinkle

PREFERENCE
apple blossom, pink geranium,
rose

PRESUMPTION
linaria, snapdragon

PRIDE
amaryllis, gloxinia,
hundred-leaved rose

PROFIT
cabbage

PROSPERITY
allium, beech tree

PROTECTION
eucalyptus, heather

PURITY
star of Bethlehem

RADIANT WITH CHARM
ranunculus

RECONCILIATION
hazel

REFINEMENT
gardenia

REGARD
daffodil

REMEMBRANCE
forget-me-not, pink carnation
(I will never forget you), rosemary

REMORSE
raspberry

RESILIENCE
chamomile (energy in adversity)

RESOLUTION
purple columbine

RESOLVE TO WIN
purple columbine

RETURN OF HAPPINESS
lily of the valley

RICHES
corn

SECRECY
maidenhair fern, peony

SECRET LOVE
honey flower

SELF LOVE
narcissus

SENSUALITY
Spanish jasmine

SEPARATION
Carolina jasmine

SINCERITY
fern, garden chervil, honesty

STRENGTH (OF CHARACTER)
fennel, ginger, gladiolus,
purple coneflower

SUCCESS
laurel

SWEETNESS
carnation (white), poppy

SYMPATHY
balm, bee balm, thrift

TEMPERANCE
azalea

TEMPTATION
apple, apple blossom, quince

TENDER RECOLLECTION
blue periwinkle

THANKFULNESS
campanula

THINK OF ME
pansy, white clover

TRANQUILITY
mudwort, stonecrop

TRUTH
anemone, chrysanthemum

UNCHANGEABLE
amaranth (globe)

VICTORY
spiraea

VIRTUE
African violet, mint, sage

WARMTH
feverfew, peppermint

WEDDED LOVE
ivy

WELCOME
wisteria

WORTH BEYOND BEAUTY
allysum

WORTHINESS
white rose

WORTHY OF ALL PRAISE
fennel

YOUR PURITY EQUALS YOUR LOVELINESS
orange blossom

YOUTHFUL GLADNESS
spring crocus

YOU WILL ALWAYS BE BEAUTIFUL TO ME
stock

ZEST
lemon blossom

BASIC MATERIALS

There is a host of tools that are helpful to have on hand when it comes to flower arranging, but in a pinch you can get by with three things: a vase, a pair of heavy sharp scissors, and some tape (Scotch tape, masking tape, or even duct tape will work). That said, there are several other supplies that come in handy that will allow for more intricate flower arranging. To stock your floral "toolbox," pick up the following: several vases (of different sizes, shapes, and depths), a floral frog (preferably a few of varying shapes and sizes), garden shears, hand clippers for the garden to cut heavy stems, thorn stripping shears (to strip the thorns off roses and other thorned stems), floral tape, floral wire (both a roll of lightweight wire for wrapping things like wreaths, and straight wire, to help flowers stand tall and to create false stems), wooden skewers, paper to wrap bouquets (butcher or kraft paper, newsprint, wrapping paper, or tissue paper), and a variety of ribbons to finish the presentation with a flourish.

SUPPORT

There is more than one way to keep flowers from listing to the side of an arrangement. The most common method is the use of a floral frog. Frogs are flat on the underside and spiky on top. When placed at the bottom of a bowl or a vase, they can hold even the most unwieldy flowers firmly upright. To use, press the ends of the stems directly onto the frog's spikes to position them exactly where you want them.

If you don't have a frog, a quick solution is to create a grid of tape across the top of the vessel in a crisscross pattern, leaving plenty of room between the lines of tape to hold stems in place. When creating the arrangement, be sure to fill in some flowers or foliage around the edges to conceal the tape.

Option number three is florist foam. Foam is not great for the environment, so it should be a last resort. To use, first soak it in water for a few hours and then place a chunk of floral foam at the bottom of your vessel and poke the stems directly into the foam.

STEM REINFORCEMENT

Sometimes getting thin, flimsy stems to stand straight is a challenge. And of course, top-heavy blooms can cause stems to bend under their weight. Fortunately, there is a simple solution to drooping stems—green floral tape. Even the most flexible stem can be made rigid with a solid wrapping of floral tape.

To apply, grasp the stem directly under the blossom. Beginning at the top of the stem, wrap floral tape around it, gradually moving downward in a spiral pattern, being sure to slightly overlap the edge of the tape. Once you've reached the bottom of the stem, cut the tape and begin wrapping the next stem in the arrangement. Another option is to place a length of floral wire alongside the stem and wrap the wire and stem together with floral tape. The two together will make even the most floppy flower stems stand soldierly.

FAKE STEMS

On occasion, an arrangement calls for a flower bloom that needs to be separated from its naturally occurring state. Gladiola blossoms are a perfect example—each stem produces many blossoms, but you may not want that many blooms so close together in an arrangement. If that's the case, you can create a "mock stem" for your bouquet using a length of floral wire and a strip of floral tape. Here's how: First remove the blossom you'd like to include from its natural stem by either cutting or pinching it off at the base of the bloom. Next, push the floral wire through the bottom of the blossom horizontally (kind of like threading a needle). Push the wire through the flower until there's an equal amount of wire on each side of the bloom, then bend both sides of the wire down to form a "stem." Then, starting at the top, directly under the flower, begin to wrap the wire "stem" with floral tape, gradually moving downward in a spiral pattern, being sure to slightly overlap the edge of the tape. When you get to the end of the wire, cut the tape. Now you have a beautiful single bloom ready to join your bouquet. When using this technique, do note that the life of that flower will be considerably shorter than one that can be arranged in water.

STEMS FOR FRUIT

Sometimes fruit makes a lovely addition to a bouquet for added meaning, a sense of abundance, extra color, and texture. But not all fruit is handily created with a stem that will seamlessly fit into a floral arrangement. If you want to include something like figs, persimmons, pomegranates, plums, pears, or any other fruit that doesn't have a long stem, all you need are thin wooden skewers. When you are ready to tuck the fruit among the flowers, simply insert the skewer into the bottom or the top (depending on which side is more visually appealing) of the piece of fruit until it reaches the core. Then tuck the skewer "stem" into the arrangement and voilà! The fruit is now part of the arrangement. If the wooden skewer is visible, wrap it in green floral tape so that it blends in with the stems of the other flowers in the bouquet.

BASHFUL BLOOMS

There are times when blooms droop, faces turned downward, as if stricken with shyness. If you find yourself working with bashful blooms, the solution is simple: all you need is a short length of floral wire and a strip of floral tape. Begin by cutting a length of floral wire to a length slightly shorter than the length of the stem. Then insert the floral wire to support the flower. Starting a few inches below the blossom's base, gently push the wire through the inside of the stem, up into the base of the flower. Next, holding the flower just below the bloom, wrap floral tape around the stem and wire to give it extra support, gradually moving downward in a spiral pattern, being sure to slightly overlap the edge of the tape. When you get to the end of the section that is supported by the wire, cut the tape or continue wrapping to the bottom of the stem.

STRIPPING STEMS

Whether using cut flowers from a garden or purchasing them from a flower market, you will most likely need to tidy the stems so they will be easy to work with and look their most elegant. If you aren't sure how much foliage you will want to leave on, retain the leaves on the top third of the stems when you do the initial pruning. Begin by removing excessive leaves and leaves that are torn, dried out, or otherwise unsightly. You can remove leaves with scissors, clippers, or thorn strippers, or by hand if they aren't too prickly. In addition, remove any thorns or prickles from the stems with either thorn strippers or hand clippers. Once the stems are cleaned up, they will be much easier to work with. You can continue to remove additional foliage as you place the stems in the bouquet.

VESSEL VARIETIES

Vases come in all shapes and sizes, and with the addition of a frog, there are no limits to what types of containers you can use for your arrangements (as long as they are watertight). Antique or contemporary teapots, such as Japanese teapots, make beautiful vessels for flower arrangements. Mason jars, ribbon- or twine-wrapped tin cans, and even watering buckets can all be gorgeously filled with blossoms. Glass, silver, stone, ceramic, and porcelain vessels all work well for lovely floral bouquets, so keep arrangements in mind when you browse through flea markets, boutique shops, or even your own kitchen.

FOLIAGE AS FILLER

When visualizing flower arrangements, remember that branches and leaves make striking additions to floral bouquets. To incorporate branches into your arrangement, simply clean up the stems as directed in the above Stripping Stems section and tuck the branches into the arrangement as desired. You can do this with branches covered in berries, young fruit, blooms, or simply gorgeous foliage.

RIBBONS AND WRAPPINGS

To give a bouquet as a gift, you can use a pretty vessel or wrap the flowers in paper or ribbon. When wrapping bouquets, be sure to use the following method: Trim the stems to the approximate length you would like for the arrangement, then lay them out on a flat surface. Next, gather several of the tallest stems and place them in the center to begin building the arrangement. Then intersperse the secondary, more delicate flowers in groupings of three that you find visually pleasing. Once the bouquet is to your liking, hold the arrangement by the stems at the base of the lowest flower blossoms and wrap all of the stems in floral tape to steady the bouquet. Trim the stems to a uniform length and then either wrap the bouquet in butcher paper or other decorative paper and tie with a ribbon, or simply wrap a ribbon around the stems and fasten it with a festive bow.

SHARE THE MEANING

When giving a bouquet infused with a meaning you want to share, be sure to include a note. The missive can be as simple and practical as a handwritten note on folded kraft paper or as elaborate as a designed and printed card that is aesthetically integrated into the bouquet. The main point is to share the meaning. After all, you've carefully chosen blooms to convey a sentiment, so be sure the recipient will remember your message long after the flowers have faded.

THE
ARRANGEMENTS

CELEBRATION

Times of joyful celebration are one of life's true pleasures. The combination
of the exuberant orange and pink poppies—"fantastic extravagance"—
and elegant white cosmos—"joy in love and life"—makes this a vibrant
bouquet that will encourage the recipient to celebrate. Create it for a job
well done, to recognize an important achievement, or even to say "Happy
Birthday." The oak leaf geranium's meaningful "friendship" is tucked in to
remind us that celebrations are even more satisfying when shared
with those we love.

poppy
FANTASTIC EXTRAVAGANCE

white cosmos
JOY IN LOVE AND LIFE

oak leaf geranium
FRIENDSHIP

1

To build this handheld bouquet, begin by holding several poppy stems in your hand. Then add the flowers one stem at a time, creating a slight spiral so there is airy space between the blossoms.

2

As you go along, mix in cosmos as is visually pleasing. Add the oak leaf geranium leaves around the edges for color and texture.

3

Trim the stems to a uniform length and place in a glass vase or jar.

TIP: Poppies will last longer if you seal the ends of the stems by quickly passing them through an open flame.

FORGIVENESS

If you need to ask someone for forgiveness or open yourself up to forgiving a hurt done to you, this delicate bouquet holds the ingredients
you need. The focus flower for "forgiveness," purple hyacinth, expresses
mercy and pardon, while raspberry vines, flowers, and buds acknowledge
the necessary emotion of "remorse" that comes with mistakes made. If
possible, add white hyacinth, meaning "beauty" to symbolize the beauty
in both forgiving and being forgiven.

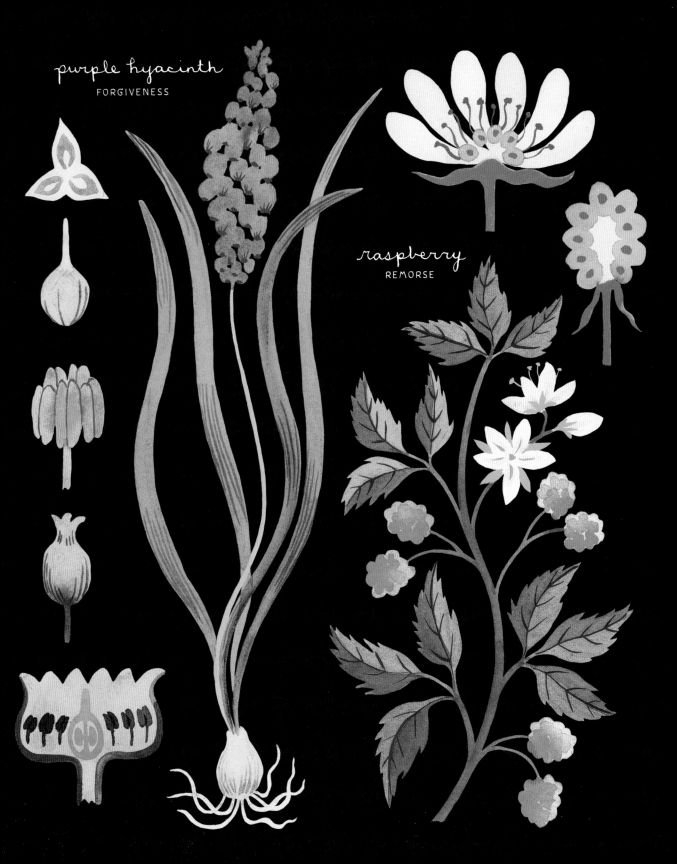

purple hyacinth
FORGIVENESS

raspberry
REMORSE

First, strip off the raspberry stem thorns with the edge of a sharp knife or thorn stripper.

Remove any leaves from the hyacinth stems and if necessary rinse any dirt off the blooms.

Begin to build the bouquet by gathering the raspberry stems. Add the hyacinth stems around the raspberry stems.

Wrap the stems with a small amount of floral tape to steady them. Trim the stems to a uniform length and then tie a ribbon around the stems to cover the tape and add a bit of flourish, or place them in a small vase.

REFINEMENT

Few flowers have the striking elegance found in the gardenia bloom, which fittingly means "refinement." Their minimalist sophistication makes gardenias a timeless favorite. In small groupings, they add a chic sensibility to décor, and their message of refined elegance makes them a great choice for lapel flowers or additions to bridal bouquets. Their heady scent adds an unexpected richness to their understated beauty.

gardenia

REFINEMENT

1

Choose several small shallow bowls of varying heights that work together aesthetically.

2

Cut a single stem of gardenia for each vase, leaving it long enough to reach the water inside. Tuck the stem into the vase so the blossom and leaves touch the lip of the vase.

3

For the single floating blooms, remove all leaves and trim the stem all the way to the base of the flower.

4

Touching only the undersides of the petals, spread the petals out and then place on top of the water in the small shallow bowls. Arrange all the vessels on a tray.

NOTE: The petals will turn brown wherever they are touched, so be careful not to touch any parts of the flower that will show in the arrangement.

BLISS

The combination of sweet pea's "blissful pleasure" and the hearty garden flower sweet William's "gallantry" along with rose of Sharon's multifaceted meanings of both "mildness" and "passion" make this the perfect bouquet to represent bliss. Create the arrangement to honor the blissful satisfaction that comes with finishing an important project, enjoying the pleasure of a lazy summer day, or the excitement of having done something outside of your comfort zone. As a gift, the bouquet will give someone you care about a symbolic pat on the back or simply invite some bliss into their days.

sweet William
GALLANTRY (DASHING COURAGE,
HEROIC BRAVERY)

rose of Sharon
MILDNESS AND PASSION

sweet pea
BLISSFUL PLEASURE

1

Choose a wide-mouthed vessel, preferably with a pedestal to give the arrangement some height.

2

Place a frog on the bottom and then insert the stiff, twiggy rose of Sharon stems one at a time to create the shape you desire. Keep the shape organic so the bouquet has a refined but natural and loose appearance.

3

Next, add the sweet pea stems to create a wave of color across the arrangement, filling in the structure created by the rose of Sharon. To add a touch of whimsy, insert several sweet pea tendrils with more on one side as a nod to the asymmetry of nature.

4

Finally, tuck in a few stems of sweet William to add texture and boldness.

CHARM

Charm means "the power of pleasing or attracting," which makes this bouquet the perfect gift for someone who has charmed you. Or create it for yourself to invite some charm into your life. The magnetic combination of characteristics that creates the quality of charm in a person is mirrored in the flower meanings entwined here. The focus flower of this arrangement—ranunculus—means "radiant with charm." The "worthiness" of the white roses is included to express the depth of character that makes one truly charming. The individual blooms of lily of the Nile—meaning "magical love"—are a unique way to include visual complexity and a sense of enchantment to the arrangement. Adding poppies—"fantastic extravagance"—makes a dazzling symbol of charm.

white rose
WORTHINESS

ranunculus
RADIANT WITH CHARM

lily of the Nile
MAGICAL LOVE

poppy
FANTASTIC EXTRAVAGANCE

1

To create the main structure, begin by taking several stems of ranunculus in your hand. When you are pleased with the way the ranunculus grouping looks, tape the stems together with floral tape so they stay in position.

2

Next, tape together the white roses in several groupings of two to three (depending on how many stems you have) and then add these groupings to the ranunculus grouping.

3

Pluck several small groupings of flowers from one to two stems of lily of the Nile and tuck them into the bouquet to add variety of color and texture while still maintaining an organic shape.

4

Finally, wrap the stems of the entire bouquet with floral tape to hold them in place. Trim the stems to a uniform length and wrap with ribbon.

PEACE

This beautiful wreath of olive branches is the quintessential peace offering. Give this wreath as a symbol of peace simply for beauty's sake or hang it on a front door to show that your home is a place of tranquility for all those who enter. Historically, evergreen wreaths have represented the forthcoming rebirth of spring when hung during the darkest days of winter. Peaceful olive branch wreaths can be adorned with colorful berries, fruit, flowers, or other foliage to bring color and a sense of festivity.

olive branches

PEACE

1

Begin with a wreath frame (available at craft stores) in the circumference size you want for the inner circle of your wreath.

2

Next gather several thin olive branches. Separate out the sprigs that have olives on them, so they can be evenly distributed once the wreath is constructed. To create the wreath, begin by making a garland of the leafy olive branches (see garland instructions, page 88) as long as needed to cover the wreath frame.

3

Then, beginning at what will be the top of the wreath, set the garland on the frame and wrap with floral wire in a spiral around both the garland and the frame, being careful to avoid the leaves so they don't get flattened.

4

Once the entire frame is covered in the olive branch garland, tuck in additional branches with olives and then attach them to the wreath frame using additional wire. If desired, tie a ribbon around the top of the wreath as a pretty hanger.

ENCHANTMENT

To be enchanted, enthralled, or entranced is to be held spellbound
by another. Give this bouquet to a special person you find enchanting
or you're hoping to enchant. At the heart of this arrangement is the
"enchantment" of the lavender roses paired with the intentionality of
pansies, Victorian-era favorites meaning "think of me" that were commonly exchanged by lovers to express longing. The "mental beauty" of
the clematis vine expresses the enchantment that comes from like minds
finding each other, while the purple columbine symbolizes one's "resolve
to win" the object of desire. Peach roses meaning "modesty" add a subtle
element, and a sprinkling of cosmos—"joy in love and life" express the
delight that enchantment brings.

lavender cabbage rose
and lavender tea rose
ENCHANTMENT

clematis
MENTAL BEAUTY

purple
columbine
RESOLVE TO WIN

pansy
THINK OF ME

peach rose
MODESTY

cosmos
JOY IN LOVE AND LIFE

When creating this bouquet, choose a vessel that is low and wide.

Add a frog that fits your vessel, or if you don't have a frog that fits, tape floral tape across the top of the vessel in a grid pattern to anchor the stems.

3

Because the lavender cabbage roses are the most striking flowers in the arrangement, begin by placing these stems to create the structure.

4

Next add the smaller lavender tea roses and then the clematis vine. When placing the clematis vine, subtly wrap it around the structure, arranging the tendrils with the flowers facing up, as they would grow toward the sun. You can also cut some of the purple columbine and clematis flowers off of the vine and tuck them into the bouquet where visually pleasing. Tuck in a few cosmos on one side of the arrangement for extra height and shape.

TIP: If your roses are more closed than you want them to be, gently blow into the bud and they will open up from the air pressure, or use your finger to gently coax the flower open, starting from the outside petals and working inward.

Finally, add the pansies in small groupings to add subtle texture and color variety.

PURE LOVE

If we are fortunate in life, we will have a few people whom we love, plain and simple. In this bouquet, daisy's "innocence" is combined with beautifully ripe strawberries meaning "perfection" because love is able to overcome our foibles and flaws. We don't have to be perfect to be loved, but both being loved and loving others brings out the best versions of ourselves. This simple bouquet is just the thing to show someone you love your gratitude and appreciation. Pure love is the greatest gift of all.

strawberry

PERFECTION

daisy

INNOCENCE

1

Begin by removing excess flowers from each daisy stem and then add the daisies to the arrangement, stem by stem, rotating the stems in a spiral pattern to allow plenty of room between the blossoms.

2

Next, intersperse the strawberry blossoms if they are in bloom throughout the bouquet, especially around the edges. If they're in season, add several large red strawberries (if they are large, you may need to create stems for them, see page 37) and lush green leaves to give the arrangement color variation.

3

Trim the stems to a uniform length, wrap them in paper, and tie the arrangement with a ribbon.

STRENGTH

In this bouquet, individual gladiolus blossoms, meaning both "strength" and "strength of character," are removed from their long stems and refashioned into single-blossom flowers to symbolize the strength found within each of us. The reshaped blooms represent the individual elements of our character that can give us the most strength when we need it. The addition of fennel, meaning "worthy of all praise," highlights the triumph we feel when we use our strength to achieve a goal. Place this arrangement in a vase or give it as a handheld bouquet to someone who has experienced an important success, or as a token of encouragement to someone who needs to stay strong through adversity.

gladiolus
STRENGTH AND STRENGTH
OF CHARACTER

fennel
WORTHY OF ALL PRAISE

1

To create this bouquet, choose the gladiolus blooms that are most open on your stems. Remove one bloom at a time from the stem by either pinching or cutting it off the stalk.

2

Next, while holding one bloom gently in your hand, poke a piece of floral wire horizontally through the bottom of the flower to create a "stem" (see Fake Stems, page 35). Place the "stem" in a jar or vessel to keep it from getting damaged while you repeat the process with as many blooms as you want for the bouquet. Creating each "stem" will take approximately two minutes once you get the hang of it, but don't worry if you fumble a bit with the first one or two attempts.

3

Once you have the desired number of "stems," add in fennel to create a natural look.

4

Either place the bouquet in a vase or wrap in paper and tie with a complementary ribbon.

THANKFULNESS

The only flower that truly expresses "thankfulness" is campanula—the variety
most commonly found is a diminutive flower too small for a bouquet,
but one that makes a sweet gift as a bunch of white or purple blooms in a
little pot. There are also larger, bell-shaped varieties that are lovely for a
bouquet, or you can combine flower meanings as we have done here for a
more visually complex arrangement. To create a statement bouquet
to express deep appreciation, combine lily of the valley's "return of
happiness" with daffodil's "regard or new beginning," and tuck in some
uplifting geranium leaves, which mean "friendship," to add color and
texture to the arrangement. (If you can't find geranium leaves, try
other greenery to add visual complexity such as star jasmine.)

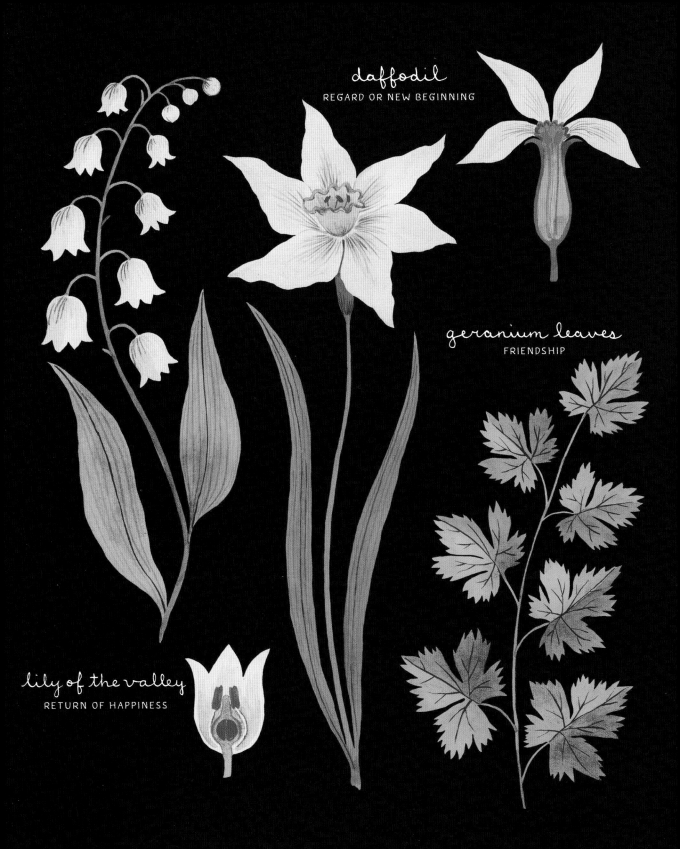

daffodil
REGARD OR NEW BEGINNING

geranium leaves
FRIENDSHIP

lily of the valley
RETURN OF HAPPINESS

1

Begin by gathering a bunch of daffodil stems in your hand. Intersperse the delicate lily of the valley stems in groupings of three as you find visually pleasing.

2

Tuck in the geranium leaves or other greenery as desired to add texture and color variation.

Wrap the stems in a small amount of floral tape to steady the bouquet. Trim the stems to a uniform length, then tuck the bouquet into a vase before delivering it to your intended.

ADORATION

The bright, lively sunflowers in this arrangement mirror the vibrant
emotion of adoration. Sunflower blooms follow the sun throughout the
day in the same way we tend to focus on the people we adore, no matter
where they are in a room. Combine dwarf sunflowers of different hues to
symbolize the fact that those we adore are admired not for just one quality, but rather for a unique combination of characteristics. (Be sure to only
use dwarf varieties, as tall sunflowers mean "haughtiness"!)

Give this bouquet to someone you adore. "Passion" is one meaning of
French marigolds (the other is "jealousy," one of the most passionate
emotions!), fitting for the fervor of adoration.

dwarf sunflower medley
ADORATION

*marigold
(red metamorph)*
PASSION

1

Choose a tall vessel that can hold several large stems but is narrow enough at the top to keep the flowers standing vertically.

2

Gather sunflowers in different shades of yellows and browns to create a rich tapestry of colors. If the blossoms of the sunflowers are drooping, use florist wire to support them (see Bashful Blooms, page 37).

3

For added visual interest, choose two to three additional sunflower stems and pluck the petals off around the center of the flower, then place alongside the other flowers in the vase. Tuck in several stems of marigolds for variety in flower sizes and textures.

4

When arranging the stems in the vase, be sure to vary the heights and directions that the blooms face to keep an organic aesthetic. However, because even cut sunflowers naturally turn toward the sunlight, their blossoms may shift throughout the day.

SUCCESS

The laurel leaf has been the symbol of success since the time of ancient Greece. It was worn as a symbol of glory and achievement by those who used their knowledge to serve the public in beneficial and honorable ways. A garland made of laurel—meaning "success"—intertwined with sage—meaning "virtue"—is the perfect decoration to adorn a home during the holidays to symbolize the success of the year past and ring in a bountiful new year. Try adding delicate flowers or berries to this arrangement for color and texture. It can also decorate a table as a festive centerpiece to ensure a successful dinner party or be hung above a door at a graduation celebration.

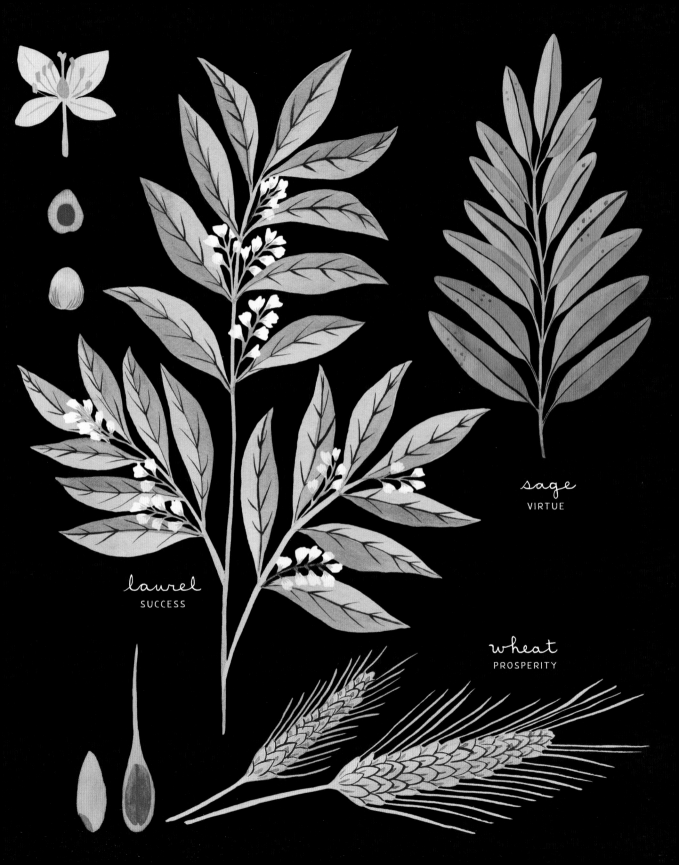

sage
VIRTUE

laurel
SUCCESS

wheat
PROSPERITY

Begin with a spool of medium-weight floral wire (the thicker the garland, the heavier the gauge needed).

Trim the stems into sections approximately 6 in/15 cm long of laurel, sage, and wheat.

To start the garland, choose a section with a nice full, leafy tip and secure the wire in the V of a leaf/stem section by twisting one end of the wire around the stem several times. This will be one end of the arrangement.

Next, stagger additional pieces (one at a time), weaving the wire in a spiral direction and avoiding the leaves so they don't get flattened. If the garland will be lying against a wall or on a flat surface, wire the stems in such a way that one side will be flat. If you're placing it where all sides will show, such as over a door or around a fireplace, be sure to wire the pieces together so that there are full leaves on all sides.

To keep the garland symmetrical, change the direction that the leaves are facing when you have reached half of the desired length. At the point where you change direction, add a decorative element, such as a ribbon, flower blossoms, or pinecones.

REMEMBRANCE

When you want to commemorate an occasion or a special person, this combination of flowers comes together for a memorable impression. Pink carnations mean "I will never forget you." Tuck in some rosemary— "remembrance"—for extra symbolism and visual depth. Small bunches of oak leaf hydrangea—meaning "dispassion" or, in this context, "calm"—can also be added for serenity. This is the perfect bouquet when the occasion calls for comforting someone whose remembrance is signified by loss.

pink
carnation
I WILL ALWAYS
REMEMBER YOU

rosemary
REMEMBRANCE

1

Begin by choosing approximately ten carnation stems (more or fewer depending on the size of your vessel). Be sure to use pink carnations because, as with roses, carnation's flower meanings vary depending on their color. Choose stems in a variety of dark and light pink hues. Strip the small leaves off the carnation stems.

2

Next, gather several stems of rosemary and strip the greenery off the bottom two-thirds of the stems, leaving greenery on the top third.

3

To assemble the bouquet, gather the carnation stems together and place them in the vessel. Next, intersperse the rosemary stems to add texture and color to the arrangement. Tuck in small bunches of oak leaf hydrangea as an optional finishing touch if you desire a little extra meaning.

TIP: Before clipping off the small flower bunches, dip the hydrangea stem in alum (a pickling ingredient that can be found in most markets) and then place it in water to help it stay fresh while you arrange the rest of the bouquet.

TRUTH

It's important to show that your sentiments are sincere. Perhaps you want to reveal your true character or be more honest with a friend. Or perhaps this arrangement symbolizes the truth of an apology or promise of commitment. The focus flower, chrysanthemum, means "truth" and provides the structural and emotional foundation. Add in the richly hued, deep purple plum leaves to symbolize your intent to keep your promises. If you are feeling like adding an extra touch of commitment to the bouquet, tuck in a few gorgeous, deep purple plums on skewers as well.

chrysanthemum
TRUTH

plum branches
KEEP YOUR PROMISES

1 Choose a short vessel with a medium-width opening and either insert a frog or crisscross floral tape across the opening of the vessel.

2 Begin with about six chrysanthemums, cleaning the stems of leaves and trimming the stems to varying lengths. Insert them one at a time and vary the directions the blossoms face to create a pleasing shape.

3 Next, add several branches of plum leaves to add visual drama and to infuse the bouquet with the importance of promises kept.

CRUSH ON YOU

The heady scent and vibrant color of orange roses—meaning "fascination"—combine with the ethereal leaves of maidenhair fern—meaning
"secrecy"—for an enchanting, lush bouquet. Rose hips—meaning "love"—
add textural beauty as well as passion. This arrangement is a lovely way
to express your feelings for someone you find fascinating. Give it to your
crush or a friend crush to let them know they've been on your mind.

orange roses and rosebuds
FASCINATION

rose hips
LOVE

maidenhair fern
SECRECY

1

Begin with a short vessel and place a frog in the bottom.

2

Select approximately fifteen orange roses of varying sizes and stages of the blooming cycle and trim off the leaves and thorns. Do the same with three to five bunches of rose hips and three to five bunches of rosebud groupings.

3

Build the arrangement by placing three roses in a triangle formation in the frog. Then, one stem at a time, fill in the arrangement with the rest of the roses, making sure to tuck blooms in around the rim of the vessel (you will need to cut the stems to the needed length so they form an organic shape).

4

Next, tuck in the groupings of rose hips and rosebud stems.

5

Finally, add sprigs of maidenhair fern to add color and texture—and a hint of secret desire.

JOY

When tulips were first introduced to Europe in the 1600s, a fervor swept the world, earning the name *tulipmania*. These irresistible flowers have inspired joy and passion ever since. Tulip meanings subtly change depending on their color, but all fall into the positive spectrum of "love" and "joy" in one form or another. These lively blossoms can be given to friends or lovers, in celebration of an event, or even as encouragement to someone who needs some extra joy and love. The addition of white jasmine's uplifting "amiability" adds texture and grace as well as a gorgeous scent.

white
jasmine
AMIABILITY

tulip
JOY AND
DECLARATION
OF LOVE

To create a luscious bouquet of cascading abundance, buy the tulips a day or two before you want to create the arrangement. They will continue to grow after they're cut, and once the stems gain length, the blossoms droop gracefully. If you prefer upright tulips, create the arrangement immediately after purchasing the flowers.

To begin, pick up the tulip stems one at a time, alternating colors as desired. Hold the stems in a loose spiral so that the blossoms have plenty of space between them.

Once the bouquet is the color combination and shape of your desire, trim the stems to a uniform length and then put them into the vase as a bunch, not stem by stem. Once the flowers are settled in the vase, move the stems around, if needed, to create your desired shape.

If you'd like to add variety and texture, as well as a pleasing scent, wrap jasmine vines around the edges of the bouquet and tuck the stems into the vase.

LUCK

The Irish are known for their luck, so it is only appropriate that the flower symbolizing good fortune is the lush green bells of Ireland. This arrangement is best presented as a bouquet wrapped in paper and tied with a gorgeous ribbon. Include some white flowering vine (such as jasmine) to add variety and texture. Give it as a gift to say "good luck"—or set it out in your own home to invite in some good old-fashioned luck o' the Irish. Add Queen Anne's lace, the delicate white flower symbolizing "fantasy," because one element of good luck is the dream— or fantasy—of wishes coming true!

bells of Ireland
LUCK

Queen Anne's lace
FANTASY

1

Begin by choosing a large bunch of bells of Ireland and cleaning up the stems by removing the lower leaves.

Then, adding one stem at a time, create a slight spiral to keep the blooms from being pressed against each other. Make sure the tips are facing in different directions so the effect is visually pleasing from all sides.

3

Once you have constructed a bouquet of your desired size, add stems of Queen Anne's lace around the outside for a sense of delicacy, texture, and the dream of success.

4

Finally, tuck in a few stems of a white flowering vine to add some textural whimsy.

5

Trim the stems to a uniform length and wrap floral tape right below the blossoms to keep them secure. Next, cut a piece of butcher paper, wrapping paper, or heavy tissue paper into a square approximately twice the size of the bouquet. Place the bouquet in the center of the paper square and gently wrap the paper around the flowers. Tie a wide cream-colored ribbon or a piece of twine around the paper to secure it, finishing off the look with a generous bow.

PASSIONATE LOVE

Whether it's desire or yearning, emotions can be all-consuming, and passionate love is the most intense of all. The primary flowers in this bouquet, red roses, focus on romantic passion. The tulip's "declaration of love" adds a layer of intentionality, and ivy's "fidelity" represents devotion. The Latin root of passion is *pati*, which means "to suffer," and sometimes suffering is what passionate love feels like—whether it's the momentary agony of being separated from one's beloved or the desperate need to touch an absent love. Embrace the tiny imperfections in the roses, such as the dry tips of the petals, because even those we passionately adore are flawed, and accepting imperfections in others is a powerful part of love.

red rose
PASSIONATE LOVE

tulip
DECLARATION OF LOVE

ivy
FIDELITY

red cabbage rose
LOVE

1

Choose a vessel with a narrow mouth so the flowers can fan out without needing a frog or other structural support.

2

Begin by placing the cabbage roses first, crisscrossing the stems to form a natural support. If possible, include flowers with slight color variations to add visual richness and complexity.

3

Next, add the red roses, continuing to crisscross the stems as you place them in the vase.

4

Intersperse tulips among the roses as is visually pleasing. Then tuck ivy stems around the bottom of the arrangement and lace them through the flowers in a way that mimics natural growth.

GRACE

The word "grace" brings to mind images of subtle beauty, a refined sense of elegance, and effortless forgiveness. This arrangement symbolizes the various facets of this powerful sentiment. Pink roses in two or three varieties, in different shades of pink, meaning "grace," are the centerpiece, with both antique cream and antique pink stock interspersed to express the lasting beauty of true grace. Grapes are draped around the edges to symbolize the abundant gratitude, gladness, and joy we feel when we are treated with grace or act gracefully in a difficult situation. Make this arrangement to welcome grace into your life or to express admiration for a graceful person you know.

champagne
grape
ABUNDANCE

antique cream
and pink stock
LASTING BEAUTY

pink rose
GRACE

Choose a vessel that is tall, slim, and elegant.

Begin by choosing three to four bunches of grapes. Trim the grape stems to approximately 1 in/2.5 cm in length; then thread a floral wire horizontally through the top of the grape stems and twist the two ends together to secure. Droop the grapes over the side with the wire "stem" inside. The grapes should simply rest there, but if they are heavy and will not stay in place, you can tape the wire "stem" to the inside of the vase.

After placing the grapes, cut several stems of stock to differing lengths and place them in the vase, leaving plenty of room between the stock flowers. Choose stock stems whose tips have interesting curves to create a graceful shape.

Add in the roses, one stem at a time, to create a sense of depth with blossom-filled nooks. Place the darker shades of pink in the depths of the arrangement and the lighter blossoms toward the front as a play on light and shadow. If possible, include several new rosebuds as well, so the bouquet can continue to evolve in its own graceful way. Because rosebuds grow toward the sun, place them in the arrangement facing up.

HAPPINESS

Delphinium's lighthearted "happiness" and bachelor button's "blessedness" intertwine to create a meaning perfectly suited for this bouquet. The stems of vibrant delphiniums can be either left tall and placed in large vessels to make a grand statement, cut down to create nosegays to adorn the table at a dinner party, or tucked into bud vases and grouped for drama. Forget-me-not's "remembrance" is interspersed to symbolize the hope that the happy moment shared will be long remembered. Any iteration of this bouquet makes a lovely hostess gift, token of friendship, or just-because surprise to bring happiness to someone's day.

delphinium
LEVITY AND HAPPINESS

bachelor button
BLESSEDNESS

forget-me-not
REMEMBRANCE

1

Begin by choosing several small glass bottles.

2

Cut several bachelor buttons and place in the bottles. Trim a few stems of forget-me-nots and add them to the arrangements.

3

Next, remove several delphinium blossoms from the large stems and intersperse them with the bachelor buttons.

4

Place the small bottles together to create an arrangement with presence.

COMFORT

Giving comfort and sympathy to others requires sensitivity and quiet reassurance, all of which are combined in this flower arrangement, created to ease the mind and cheer the soul. Dahlias, meaning "dignity," remind us that there is dignity even during times of distress. "Comfort" is symbolized by scarlet geranium leaves, meaning "sympathy." Globe amaranth, meaning "unchangeable," is included to remind us that even during difficult times, we can count on the unchangeable presence of friends and family for loving support.

scarlet
geranium leaves
COMFORT

globe
amaranth
UNCHANGEABLE

dahlia
DIGNITY

Begin by choosing a vessel that is sturdy and has a wide mouth.

Insert a frog or crisscross floral tape across the top to support the stems. Begin with fifteen to twenty dahlias in a variety of complementary colors. Insert three tall stems in a triangle formation, then trim the remaining dahlia stems to differing lengths and fill in the triangle with flowers of varying heights. Be sure to face the blooms in several directions and tuck some of the dahlias around the lip of the vessel.

Intersperse globe amaranth through the middle of the arrangement for a vertical element.

Finally, tuck a few geranium leaves around the bottom for a pleasant drooping effect, as well as in the middle of the bouquet for added color and texture.

I AM PROUD OF YOU

Giving someone an amaryllis is akin to offering a champagne toast—
a gesture to celebrate success or show how proud you are. The dramatic
amaryllis, meaning "pride," is a striking centerpiece to express that
sentiment. Singularly spectacular—and available in white, red, dusky
peach, or striped—these flowers can be grown from bulbs or given as
dramatic cut arrangements. Amaryllis can be purchased year-round at
markets that import flowers from Holland but are especially available
in bulb form in the fall at most garden stores. For an exquisite impression,
combine several types of amaryllis in one vase. The purple columbine
leaves—meaning "resolution"—are incorporated as a nod to the resolve
it often takes to achieve an important goal.

columbine leaves
RESOLUTION

amaryllis
PRIDE

1

For a cut arrangement, begin by selecting a sturdy vase with a wide opening and placing a frog inside.

2

Trim the stems to the desired length and press them into the frog. If the heavy blooms cause the arrangement to lean, fill the vessel with pebbles for support.

3

Tuck stems of purple columbine leaves around the edges to add varied color and texture as well as depth of meaning.

MATERNAL LOVE

A mother's love surrounds her child. It is steadfast and faithful. In this arrangement, maternal love is symbolized by the moss's warm, blanketing presence surrounding an African violet, which means "virtue," because there is no love more virtuous than the love between a mother and child. Purple violets in particular mean "filled with love," making this the perfect arrangement to celebrate the purity of a mother's unconditional love. The protective cloche replicates the intimate, sometimes insular nature of the mother-child relationship and adds something special to this gift, perfect for new or expectant mothers or for Mother's Day.

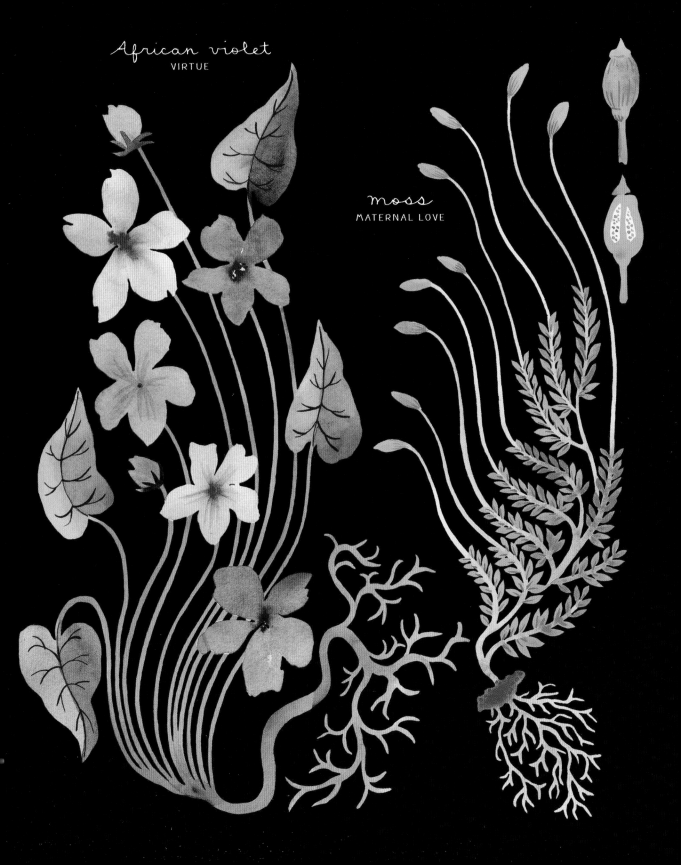

African violet
VIRTUE

moss
MATERNAL LOVE

1

Plant a violet plant in a small pot or vessel with a hole on the bottom for drainage.

2

Firmly pack moss around the base of the violet.

3

Place the arrangement on a small plate or tray and cover with a glass cloche.

NOTE: Water the plant slightly less than instructed by the planting recommendations, because the cloche will act as a miniature greenhouse and retain moisture. If the plant is not thriving, remove the cloche temporarily and allow the soil to dry before watering the plant again.

MISS YOU

If you are pining for that certain someone, need to reconcile with an important person in your life, or just want to express feelings of missing a friend, this combination of flowers creates a meaningful arrangement to say "I miss you." The focus flower, zinnia, means both "thoughts of you" and "I mourn your absence," while Carolina jasmine meaning "separation" symbolizes thoughts about the person missed. If you can't find Carolina jasmine, add another green vine for color. Tuck in a few stems of salvia, meaning "esteem," to show the importance of the missed person.

sage (salvia)
ESTEEM

zinnia
THOUGHTS OF YOU,
I MOURN YOUR ABSENCE

Carolina jasmine
SEPARATION

1

Select a vertical vase and place a frog inside to secure the flower stems.

2

Choose zinnias in several shades of complementary colors and trim the stems to varying lengths. Place the three tallest stems in a triangle formation to establish the structure of the arrangement. Next, fill in the triangle with more zinnias and a few stems of salvia until the bouquet is lush and full.

Once the zinnias are arranged, tuck in several stems of green vine, letting the tendrils droop over the sides and gently wrapping the vine around the base of the vase. Place one or two stems of vine in the middle of the arrangement as well to fill out the shape of the arrangement.

BRAVERY

Sometimes people we care about need extra encouragement to be boldly brave. Whether they are struggling with an ailment, getting through an emotionally difficult time, or taking on a physical feat that requires an extra serving of plucky audacity, serving up a gorgeous dose of encouragement is exactly what is needed to help dear ones courageously and victoriously conquer what is in front of them. The daring, spirited peony— meaning "bravery"—provides a stunning show of strength to get the job done. If you can't find willow branches, add another green vine for more color and texture.

peony
BRAVERY

willow
branches
BRAVERY

1

Select a vertical vase and place a frog inside to secure the flower stems.

2

Choose an abundant quantity of peonies in several shades of complementary colors and trim the stems to varying lengths. Place the three tallest stems in a triangle formation to establish the structure of the arrangement. Next, fill in the triangle with more peonies until the bouquet is lush and full.

3

Once the peonies are arranged, tuck in several stems of green vine, letting the tendrils droop over the sides and gently wrapping the vine around the base of the vase. Place one or two stems of willow branches or other green vine in the arrangement as well to fill out the shape of the arrangement.

RESOURCES

The flowers in this book were plucked (for the most part) from the gorgeous array of blossoms found in the San Francisco Flower Market, and the resources noted here are heavily represented within those four walls.

Neighborhood farmers' markets are always a wonderful place to find fresh, seasonal flowers. Flower nurseries are also a terrific place to purchase flowering plants that can be used in bouquets and then planted in your garden so you can grow flowers to use later. And, of course, your local florists, neighborhood flower stands, and often even flea markets have bountiful flowers for sale.

If you are in the mood for a floral adventure, you can always forage for flowers where foraging is allowed, or become friends with your neighbors who have thriving flower gardens in hopes that they are willing to share.

ALAMEDA FLEA MARKET
www.alamedapointantiquesfaire.com
2900 Navy Way (at Main Street)
Alameda, CA 94501
First Sunday of every month

AMAZON
www.amazon.com
Of course this site has everything, including Felco shears (the best shears), a floral holster, vases, and floral tape.

BRANNAN STREET WHOLESALE FLORIST
www.brannanst.com
634 Brannan Street
San Francisco, CA 94107
415.986.7740

COAST WHOLESALE FLORIST
www.coastwholesaleflorist.com
149 Morris Street
San Francisco, CA 94107
415.777.8533

GARCIA GREENS
www.garciagreens.com
640 Brannan Street
San Francisco, CA 94107
415.866.7004

HIGHLIGHT RENTALS AND HIGHLIGHT TOO
www.highlightrentals.com
640 Brannan Street
San Francisco, CA 94107
415.495.3780

LASSEN RANCH FLOWERS
644 Brannan Street
San Francisco, CA 94107
415.546.3818

MICHAELS
www.michaels.com
Lots of craft supplies, floral wire, tapes, kraft paper, and inexpensive glass vases.

REPETTO'S GREENHOUSE FLORIST
www.repettosgreenhouseflorist.com
644 Brannan Street
San Francisco, CA 94107
415.543.2529

SLOW FLOWERS
http://slowflowers.com
A national directory to organic flower farms all over the country.

TERRAIN
www.shopterrain.com
For all things garden-related: planters, tools, and gardening supplies.

TORCHIO NURSERY
www.torchionursery.com
640 Brannan Street #87
San Francisco, CA 94107
415.543.8035

BIBLIOGRAPHY

Adams, H. G. *The Language and Poetry of Flowers*. Philadelphia: J. B. Lippincott, 1864.

Diffenbaugh, Vanessa. *The Language of Flowers*. New York: Ballantine/Random House, 2011.

Kleager, Brenda Jenkins. *The Secret Meaning of Flowers: Including Trees, Shrubs, Vines and Herbs*. Huntsville, AL: Treasured Secrets Publishing, 2013.

Pickston, Margaret. *The Language of Flowers*. New York: Viking Press, 1987. Originally published in 1913.

Scoble, Gretchen and Ann Field. *The Meaning of Flowers: Myth, Language, and Lore*. San Francisco: Chronicle Books, 1998.

ACKNOWLEDGMENTS

First and foremost, we would like to thank Leslie Jonath for bringing together the amazing team who have so lovingly worked on this book. A big thank-you to the Chronicle Books creatives, including editor Laura Lee Mattingly for starting us off and then Sara Golski for jumping in at the eleventh hour to finish the job. Lots of gratitude goes out to the visionary designer, Allison Weiner, who brought her gorgeous design sensibility to the project and lured the talented Annabelle Breakey on board to add her impeccable photographic eye. Thank you to Vikki Chu for the exquisite watercolor illustrations. A huge thank-you goes to Max Gill for letting us pilfer his studio and garden for many of the vessels and blooms in this book. Thank you to Simone Chezar for her help on and off the set. Last but not least, a big thank-you to Kristi Hein for her thoughtful and detailed copyedit. Many stems of campanula to you all!

INDEX

"Adoration," 82–85
amaranth (globe), 11, 122, 123
amaryllis, 11, 126, 127

Bachelor button, 11, 118, 119
basic materials, 34
bells of Ireland, 11, 106, 107
"bliss," 54–57
blooms, bashful, 37
"bravery," 138–41

Carnation, 12, 90, 91
"celebration," 42–45
"charm," 58–61
chrysanthemum, 12, 94, 95
clematis, 12, 66, 67
columbine, 12, 66, 67, 126, 127
"comfort," 122–25
cosmos, 12, 42, 43, 66, 67
"crush on you," 98–101

Daffodil, 15, 78, 79
dahlia, 15, 122, 123
daisy, 15, 70, 71
delphinium, 15, 118, 119

"Enchantment," 66–69

Fennel, 15, 74, 75
flower glossaries
    by flower meaning, 26–31
    by flower name, 10–25
flowers
    with bashful blooms, 37
    fake stems for, 35
    reinforcing stems of, 35
    seasonal, 7
    sources of, 142
    stripping stems of, 38
    supporting, 34, 37
foam, floral, 34
foliage, as filler, 38
forget-me-not, 15, 118, 119
"forgiveness," 46–49
frogs, 34
fruit, stems for, 37

Gardenia, 15, 50, 51
geranium, 15, 42, 43, 78, 79,
    122, 123
gladiolus, 16, 74, 75
"grace," 114–17
grape, 16, 114, 115

"Happiness," 118–21
hyacinth, 16, 46, 47
hydrangea, 16, 90

"I am proud of you," 126–29
ivy, 16, 110, 111

Jasmine
    Carolina, 16, 134, 135
    white, 16, 102, 103
"joy," 102–5

Laurel, 19, 86, 87
lily of the Nile, 19, 58, 59
lily of the valley, 19, 78, 79
"luck," 106–9

Maidenhair fern, 19, 98, 99
marigold, 19, 82
"maternal love," 130–33
meanings
    flower glossary by, 26–31
    multiple, 7
    season and, 7
    sharing, 39
"miss you," 134–37
moss, 19, 130, 131

Notes, 39

Olive, 20, 62, 63

Pansy, 20, 66, 67
"passionate love," 110–13
"peace," 62–65
peony, 20, 138, 139
plum, 20, 94, 95
poppy, 20, 42, 43, 58, 59
"pure love," 70–73

Queen Anne's lace, 20, 106, 107

Ranunculus, 20, 58, 59
raspberry, 20, 46, 47
"refinement," 50–53
"remembrance," 90–93
ribbons, 39
rosemary, 23, 90, 91
rose of Sharon, 23, 54, 55
roses
    hips, 23, 98, 99
    lavender, 23, 66, 67
    orange, 23, 98, 99
    peach, 23, 66, 67
    pink, 23, 114, 115
    red, 23, 110, 111
    white, 23, 58, 59

Sage, 23, 86, 87, 134
stems
    fake, 35
    for fruit, 37
    reinforcing, 35
    stripping, 38
stock, 23, 114, 115
strawberry, 23, 70, 71
"strength," 74–77
"success," 86–89
sunflower, 23, 82, 83
support, 34, 37
sweet pea, 24, 54, 55
sweet William, 24, 54, 55

Tape, floral, 34, 35
"thankfulness," 78–81
tools, 34
"truth," 94–97
tulip, 24, 102, 103, 110, 111

Vases and other vessels, 38
violet (African), 24, 130, 131

Wheat, 24, 87
willow, 24, 138, 139
wrappings, 39

Zinnia, 24, 134, 135

gladiolus
STRENGTH AND STRENGTH
OF CHARACTER

daf
REGARD OR

rosemary
REMEMBRANCE

fennel
WORTHY OF ALL PRAISE